Touchstones for Prayer

William P. Roberts

Touchstones for Prayer

- Abraham
- Moses
- Jeremiah
- Jesus
- Paul
- Mary

Nihil Obstat:
   Rev. Hilarion Kistner, O.F.M.
   Rev. John J. Jennings

Imprimi Potest:
   Rev. Jeremy Harrington, O.F.M.
   Provincial

Imprimatur:
   Rev. John L. Cavanaugh, V.G.
   Archdiocese of Cincinnati
   April 5, 1983

The *Nihil Obstat* and *Imprimatur* are a declaration that a book or pamphlet is considered to be free from doctrinal or moral error. It is not implied that those who have granted the *Nihil Obstat* and *Imprimatur* agree with the contents, opinions or statements expressed.

Scripture passages so indicated are taken from the *New American Bible*, copyright © 1970, by the Confraternity of Christian Doctrine, Washington, D.C., and are used by permission of the copyright owner. All rights reserved.

All other Scripture texts are excerpts from *The Jerusalem Bible*, copyright © 1966 by Darton, Longman & Todd, Ltd. and Doubleday & Company, Inc. Used by permission of the publisher.

Excerpts from the English translation of *The Roman Missal* © 1973, International Committee on English in the Liturgy, Inc. All rights reserved.

Book design and cover by Julie Lonneman.

SBN 0-86716-023-3

© 1983, William P. Roberts
St. Anthony Messenger Press
All rights reserved.
Printed in the U.S.A.

*This book is dedicated
in loving gratitude
to Mildred O'Hearn,
my friend and mother-in-law.*

Acknowledgments

I wish to thank my wife Challon for her support and insightful help through the various stages of composing this book.

I am grateful to Karen Hurley and Carol Luebering, editors at St. Anthony Messenger Press, for their guidance and careful editing.

My thanks also go to three of my colleagues who read an earlier draft of the manuscript and provided many valuable suggestions: Vincent Branick, Professor of New Testament, University of Dayton; Rev. James Heft, S.M., Professor of Systematic Theology, University of Dayton; and Rev. Gregory Tajchman, O.F.M., former Professor of Old Testament, Mt. St. Mary's Seminary.

Finally, I wish to express my appreciation to my typists, Joanne Beirise, Joyce Detzel and Suzanne Ksycewski.

Contents

Introduction   2

Part one
    The prayer of our ancestors:
    Abraham, Moses and Jeremiah

Chapter one: 'To the land I will show you'   6

Chapter two: 'Go to the pharaoh'   16

Chapter three: 'Woe is me!'   27

Part two
    The prayer of Jesus

Chapter four: 'Abba, Father'   38

Chapter five: 'The Word was made flesh'   45

Chapter six: 'By their fruits...'   52

Chapter seven: 'Like a grain of wheat'   62

Chapter eight: 'Teach us to pray'   74

Part three
    The prayer of disciples:
    Paul and Mary

Chapter nine: 'Through him, with him, in him'   82

Chapter ten: 'According to your Word'   89

Epilogue   97

Introduction

When the disciples begged Jesus for lessons in prayer, they expressed an anxiety as old as belief: How should we pray? They chose a wise course in bringing their question to Jesus. For no one can speak to our anxiety as well as a truly prayerful person.

This book follows the disciples' lead. It turns not only to Jesus, but to five other persons whose prayer, recorded in Scripture, speaks with extraordinary immediacy to our own experience. These six faced the same roadblocks to prayer we struggle with today; they exploded the misconceptions that still confuse our attempts at prayer. Is there a way they can help us?

Before chemistry was a science, alchemists gauged the purity of precious metals by the streak they left when rubbed against a *touchstone*. In the same sense, these biblical pray-ers are offered here as touchstones for contemporary pray-ers. In this book, we will touch our experience to theirs and let the insights they gained in prayer test the integrity of our own prayer life.

Part I looks to the Old Testament where we find ourselves in the company of three prayerful people: Like *Abraham* we find ourselves called in prayer to a land we do not know. Like *Moses* we discover that prayer cannot remain neatly isolated in a corner of our lives; it bids us challenge the pharaohs of our day and engage in the troublesome task of liberating ourselves and others from injustice. Like *Jeremiah* we learn that prayer is a two-edged sword: at times a source of delight and joy, at other times impelling us to cry out, "Woe is me!"

Then our quest for touchstones takes us to the New Testament. In Part II we linger in the company of the one in whose name we pray: *Jesus Christ*. Like Jesus, we experience prayer not as an encounter with a distant and abstract God, but with One who can be addressed in intimate terms as "*Abba*, Father." We explore the significance the Incarnation has for praying people who are by nature enfleshed. We probe the interlacement of prayer and action in the life of Jesus and find some startling implications. We sense the paschal dimension of our prayer and turn, like the disciples, to Jesus for explicit instruction in the art of prayer.

Finally, Part III introduces us to the prayer of the first Christian disciples. Like *Paul* we discover that Christian faith places the risen Lord at the center of life and prayer. Like *Mary* we perceive that the core meaning of our prayer is radical openness to God's Word even where we do not understand all the implications.

The prayer of our ancestors: Abraham, Moses and Jeremiah

Chapter one

'To the land I will show you'

Yahweh said to Abram, "Leave your country, your family and your father's house, for the land I will show you. I will make you a great nation; I will bless you and make your name so famous that it will be used as a blessing.

"I will bless those who bless you:
I will curse those who slight you.
All the tribes of the earth
shall bless themselves by you."

So Abram went as Yahweh told him....
(Genesis 12:1-4)

Often-heard comments about prayer are very telling: "I am praying very hard so that God will hear me." "I prayed and prayed, but God did not answer." Such statements reveal an image of a God who is very distant from our human situation. Prayer to such a God is something *we* must initiate in order to make God aware of our needs. *We* set the agenda. Then, if we pray hard enough, perhaps God will respond and cooperate in our designs.

Thephrase prayer of our Hebrew ancestors, on the other hand, reveals a very different understanding: For the pray-ers we meet in the Old Testament, God takes the initiative. God first communicates to us; we are then enabled to respond. God sets the agenda; we are challenged to listen. In following God's design for us, we find life. Prayer, from this scriptural view, is our human response to a God who is already communicating to us. A striking example of this understanding of prayer is found in Abraham's story in the first book of the Hebrew Scriptures.

Abraham lived in the Near East about 19 centuries before Christ. His neighbors believed there were many gods responsible for different aspects of nature—agricultural gods, storm gods, fertility gods, to mention a few. The devotees of these gods performed magical rituals to compel the gods to fulfill human demands.

It was against this religious background that Abraham received a new faith-understanding of God. In some kind of extraordinary prayer experience Abraham perceived God as the one Being ultimately responsible for all creation. This God chose to become personally involved in Abraham's history and in the history of his people.

This new view of God, received in faith and prayer, had serious implications for Abraham. He had to give up and leave behind many of the cherished beliefs and religious practices of his ancestors, his family and his friends. This leaving is concretely symbolized by Abraham's physical departure for a land which God would show him.

There, God promised, Abraham would become the father of a great people. Abraham believed in the promise even though it seemed his wife was incapable of having children.

Prayer: God's initiative

God's initiative in prayer comes through clearly in the description of one of Abraham's religious experiences (see Genesis 15:7-21). This description must be placed in the context of an ancient ritual of covenant in which an animal was cut in two and the halves placed opposite each other. The contracting parties then passed between the parts of the slain animal and called down upon themselves the fate that befell the animal should they violate the agreement. In Abraham's religious encounter he prepares a young cow, a goat and a ram for such a ritual. A smoking brazier and a flaming torch then pass between them.

As is often the case in Scripture, fire is used as a symbol of God. The significance of the narrative is that God takes the initiative and enters into covenant with Abraham and his descendants. Only God walks between the halves; Abraham does not. The covenant between God and Abraham is unilateral. It is God's creation and does not depend on any human.

The biblical description of Abraham's call illustrates an essential element for understanding our own experience of prayer: God's self-communication to us is the foundation of our prayer life. Without God's gift of grace, we have no faith, we have no spiritual yearning, we have no desire to pray. The longings we have for Someone beyond ourselves, for a more perfect love, for a better prayer life—these are signs that God has *already* touched us and is *already* calling us.

Unlike Abraham, most of us have never been "swept off our feet" by some overwhelming religious experience accompanied by extraordinary signs. God's communication rarely comes in such a manner. Yet God communicates to us daily through creation—through the sweep of the universe and, in a particular way, through our own uniqueness. God speaks to us through the Scriptures and through the faith our community hands on to us even to this day. God is with us in our evolving history, communicating the Spirit to us in the innermost depths of our hearts and through our intimate relationships with others. As with Abraham God is already calling us, touching us, *before* we respond.

In the Abraham narrative, fire signifies God's presence. It is an appropriate symbol. Fire gives light and heat. It makes radiant and transforms. So God does to us. When we pray we do so because the Spirit of truth and love is already present within us. God *already* knows us, favors us and is committed to us in faithful love. When we pray, we allow God to empower us, to transform us and warm us with compassionate love.

Since God initiates the process of prayer, we need not struggle or be apprehensive. There is no reason to strain or to try too hard. We need but *respond* to the call to enter into communion and friendship with God.

Prayer is listening to God. It is following God's movement within us. It is becoming attuned to God's perception of us and of the whole world. It is believing that we are worthwhile because of who we are in God's sight, not because of what we accomplish. Prayer involves letting go of ourselves and allowing God's spirit to transform us.

The value of our prayer, then, cannot be measured in terms of *our* efforts, or by the "success" of our attempts at prayer. Our desire to pray is already a response to God's action and, hence, already a prayer—even when distractions carry our attention away or sleep overcomes us. The value of prayer is the immeasurable transformation of our minds and hearts that takes place whenever we respond to the God who is forever committed to us.

Beyond our present horizons

We usually experience a certain uneasiness, even pain, whenever we must depart. Leaving home, finishing school, going to a new job—moving on always involves surrendering what is familiar, saying goodbye to people we love and giving up a certain amount of security.

The excitement of going to a new place is at least partially overshadowed by loneliness, a sense of loss and the anxiety about the unknown dimensions of the future. "Will it be worth it?" "Would I be better off staying where I am?" "Will the suffering involved bring greater happiness and personal fulfillment?"

One of the reasons we are sometimes reluctant to pray is that prayer opens up new horizons in our understanding of God and ourselves. We can never be sure what responding to God will call forth in our life. We surely will not be bidden to stand still, but to venture ahead. Knowing this fills us with fear; it is a challenge to believe in God's repeated promise, "I am with you." Our faith meets a test. To pray, to say yes, is to move forward. To move forward is to inscribe our prayer more deeply into our lives.

In our prayer we tend to restrict God to what, in our narrow view, seems good for us. In Abraham's experience of prayer, the opposite took place. God presented to Abraham a vision of the future that went beyond his wildest dreams. To be open to that future, Abraham had to surrender his own plans. He had to believe that what God proposed was, despite all the difficulties, better for him. He had to embark on a journey without knowing where it would lead.

The prayer experience of Abraham speaks to every age because it is such a dramatic example of the "leaving" that faith and prayer so often involve. Across the centuries we can feel how painful it is when children abandon their parents' religious beliefs. We can imagine the loneliness of following a path of religious faith unsupported by friends and peers. When we reflect on Abraham's experience in light of what this kind of leaving would mean to us personally, we can sense the suffering involved. We can also perceive more keenly the strength of Abraham's faith and the price he was willing to pay in order to be true to his God.

The call to leave and the challenge to believe

in a God who promises us a new future are integral to our prayer life. At times such leaving is connected with the ordinary human passages that take place in our own development and that of our loved ones. Moving from childhood to adolescence, then to adulthood, the middle years and old age involves both separation from the familiar and a bold step into an uncertain future.

Some journeys begin with a free choice: to marry, to have another child, to embrace a second career or become involved in a new ministry. In such choices we take a radical step that affects our life-style and commits us to a new course. Other leavings are imposed by loss, separations not of our choosing.

In prayer we are asked to offer the pain of all of these leavings. We are called to trust that the abiding presence of God will guide us into the unseen future and provide us with all we need for the journey.

The ultimate culmination of our prayer life is the end of our journey on this earth. All of the leavings we make with trust in God's promise prepare us for the final moment of death. Death challenges us to let go of all that we know and cherish in this world with a final, total act of faith and trust. We are invited to abandon ourselves freely into the "hands" of a God who, we believe, will meet us face to face "on the other side." This is our ultimate prayer of hope and love. In a way, this prayer is contained in all our earlier moments of prayer. In another way, all those earlier moments of prayer are caught up into this final and total prayer.

New ethical challenges

Abraham's experience of God led him far from home to a new life in a strange land. It led him to the joy of fatherhood when Isaac, the child promised by God, was born to brighten his old age. And it led him to a further test of his faith, a crisis more severe than he ever could have imagined.

> It happened some time later that God put Abraham to the test. "Abraham, Abraham," he called. "Here I am," he replied. "Take your son," God said, "your only child Isaac, whom you love, and go to the land of Moriah. There you shall offer him as a burnt offering, on a mountain I will point out to you." (Genesis 22:1-2)

Ancient Near Eastern peoples practiced child sacrifice. They believed that offering the life of one's own children was appeasing to the gods. Abraham, at first, believed that his God also wished the supreme sacrifice of his son. As long as this was his conviction, he had the faith to offer his son willingly.

Abraham was to learn differently. Just as he raised the knife to sacrifice the boy, a voice from heaven stayed his hand. Through God's own revelation, Abraham discovered that this God did not desire the death of a child. Abraham's newly discovered God was a God of life, a God of people. Abraham again had faith—enough faith to be open to this discovery. Consequently he abandoned the thought of sacrificing Isaac.

Abraham's religious experience led him to a new perception of what God demands and does not demand from humans. The same experience can occur in our own prayer life. As we pray, we grow in our appreciation of who we are. We also grow in our experience of God's love and in our understanding of how this love is to be translated into our actions and into our relationships with one another.

This gradual growth occasionally brings about a dramatic shift in the way we view our moral responsibilities and the appropriateness of our religious practices. Certain actions we once thought God demanded from us then cease to seem part of God's will. On the other hand, we become sensitive to new obligations emerging from our faith in God, responsibilities which earlier we had overlooked.

Discovering what God is really asking of us is an important aspect of our prayer. Sometimes we must put aside certain actions we once thought consonant with God's will. In former eras, for example, Christians presumed that owning slaves, burning heretics at the stake and killing "pagan" natives in new-found lands were consistent with God's will. Today such behavior is incompatible with our belief in the universal parenthood of God. Prior to Vatican II many people thought it was God's law that believers fast from midnight before receiving the Eucharist and abstain from meat on Friday. Today we have come to see social responsibilities as far more central to Christian discipleship than certain acts of individual piety. We have become more sensitive to the fact that an essential dimension of God's will for us is to assuage suffering in the human family, to relieve the starvation, ignorance and institutionalized oppression of our sisters and brothers.

If our prayer life is vibrant, our consciences will be sensitized. It will become apparent that what we have been doing "in the name of the Lord" is not enough, that what we believed to be God's will was possibly wrong or, at least, irrelevant to what God really demands. This realization need not lead to guilt. It can, rather, help shake us out of complacency. It can lead us toward a more intense search for what God is asking of us today. With greater humility and a more generous openness to God, we listen, willing to respond to new challenges as they gradually unfold before us.

Conclusion

Prayer is a living reality. It is not something we do to move God. Prayer happens because God is moving us. We pray when we respond in word and action to the transforming power of God, who is ever leading us beyond our present toward a fuller life and the more demanding challenges of love.

Touchstones

- In your prayer do you *allow* God to speak first?
- Do you wait for the Lord to speak your name, to call you to new, unexplored territory?
- Where is God calling you now?
- What must you leave behind in order to go forth?

Chapter two

'Go to the pharaoh'

And Yahweh said, "I have seen the miserable state of my people in Egypt. I have heard their appeal to be free of their slave-drivers. Yes, I am well aware of their sufferings. I mean to deliver them out of the hands of the Egyptians and bring them up out of that land to a land rich and broad, a land where milk and honey flow,...so come, I send you to Pharaoh to bring the sons of Israel, my people, out of Egypt." (Exodus 3:7-8,10)

In our efforts to pray, we can easily fall victim to any number of damaging tendencies. But the story of Moses and his prayer can offer us corrective insights regarding these self-defeating attitudes:

A sense of inferiority. We are inclined to think that a person really has to be "holy" to have a serious prayer life. With full knowledge of our sins and imperfections, we therefore judge ourselves incapable of any deep experience of God.

Praying in isolation. We often cut ourselves off from the long history of God's communication with others. We easily forget that our prayerful perception of God is filtered through the faith of many who have gone before us as well as through the faith of our contemporaries.

Controlling God. It is so tempting to reduce God to a neat and clear definition. We would like to have a tightly-knit package of answers that would tell us all there is to know about God. God would then become predictable—and controllable.

Divorcing prayer from life. If only we could keep our prayer separate from our responsibility to confront the harsh realities of our everyday life! We are particularly reluctant to let our prayer inspire and empower us to challenge the people who try to oppress us.

The religious experience of Moses can help us face and overcome all four of the above.

Moses lived in the 13th century before Christ. His Hebrew ancestors had settled in Egypt during the time of Joseph, about five centuries earlier. By Moses' time official Egyptian attitudes toward the Hebrews had changed and forced them into slavery.

Early in his life Moses was revealed as a man of compassion. When he saw an Egyptian strike a Hebrew, he killed the attacker on the spot. When he realized his act had been seen, he fled for his life into Midian. Scarcely had he arrived there when he saw some shepherds drive away seven women who had come to a well to draw water for their flock. He immediately went to the women's defense and watered their flock for them (see Exodus 2:11-17).

This was the man God called to the difficult

task of leading his people from slavery to freedom: one who had already shown himself willing to take risks to defend the oppressed.

As Moses tended his father-in-law's flock, God spoke to him from the middle of a burning bush. The God of Abraham, Isaac and Jacob, having witnessed the suffering of the Hebrews, was sending Moses to the pharaoh to demand their release. In response to this call, Moses championed the cause of freedom. Despite the obstacles presented by the obstinacy of the Egyptians, despite his own people's frequent grumbling and lack of cooperation, Moses pursued the lifelong task of freeing the Israelites from slavery and leading them to a life of new promise.

Who is worthy?

By human standards Moses, on the surface at least, seems an unlikely candidate for an extraordinary religious experience and a divine call. He was a fugitive from the law, wanted for murder. With that kind of record he would have grave difficulty being admitted to any contemporary religious community or to any leadership role in today's parish. God, however, saw beyond the *facts* about Moses into the *person*. God saw a man who was passionate for justice, a suitable instrument for God's design for the liberation of the Hebrew people.

God always sees beyond externals into the human heart. He perceives not merely our faults and sinful inclinations but, more importantly, our strengths and talents. God sees our potential for good as well as our potential for evil. If we are to avoid underestimating our ability to pray, we need to see and accept ourselves as God does. We need to believe that God empowers us and calls us to enter into a personal relationship with him.

Only then can we trust ourselves and be open to God's transforming action within us. This kind of perception keeps us from putting limits on our potential for growth in prayer. It makes it possible to listen responsively to whatever God summons forth from us.

This belief that God looks beyond externals into the human heart must also make us cautious not to prejudge the prayer life of other people. Do we find it hard to believe that people who don't go to church nevertheless pray a great deal? Are we surprised to discover that a patient in a hospital for the emotionally and mentally disturbed has an authentic life of deep faith and prayer? Are we shocked to learn of a prostitute who very much believes in God's presence and love?

The God of our ancestors

"I am the God of your father, the God of Abraham, the God of Isaac and the God of Jacob" (Exodus 3:6), God tells Moses. In other words, God does not communicate to Moses in an historical vacuum. While Moses has an extraordinary religious experience that places unique demands on him, his perception of God does not occur in isolation from the faith of his ancestors. The God he encounters is the same God who spoke to Abraham, Isaac and Jacob. Their faith-understanding, passed on down through the generations, serves as an important context for Moses' own personal insights into God.

In order to understand how God communicates to us in prayer today, we need to avoid two extremes. One extreme says the community's faith tradition is irrelevant to life today. It assumes God speaks to a person in an individualistic way, and that the faith perceptions of others, especially people from the past, have no significance for that person's interpretation of God's message. The other extreme limits God's communication to the past. It insists God has no more to say to humans than what is already in the Bible or cherished in the past tradition of the Church. To receive God's communication, one need only go to these storehouses.

Between these two extremes is a middle ground: God continues to speak to us in our present history, but does so in the context of the faith tradition passed on through the community. The Spirit of God dwells within each of us, enabling us to recall what has been spoken to our ancestors in faith and to understand what is being communicated through the living community of believers today. The Spirit guides each of us in applying this living Word to the unique circumstances and demands of our own situation.

For growth in prayer, it is important to read Scripture and to know how it has been interpreted and passed down through the ages. It is also important to learn how the Scriptures are being applied by the faith community to the changing circumstances of today's world. In this light each of us can allow the Spirit to inspire us to embrace whatever God is asking in our lives.

Beyond our grasp

Prostrate before the burning bush, Moses asks God the question that people of faith have been posing for millennia: What is God's name? The answer, "I Am who I Am" (Exodus 3:14), is significant.

Much scholarly dispute centers on the meaning of this name. One interpretation presented in the *Jerusalem Bible* suggests that "I Am who I Am" indicates it is impossible to give an adequate definition of God. In Semitic thought knowing a name gave power over the thing named. Knowing the name of a god gave one the ability to call on that god and be certain of a hearing. The God of Abraham, Isaac and Jacob refuses to become anyone's slave in this way and declines to reveal a name that expresses the divine essence. Understood in this way, the answer to Moses' question emphasizes God's *transcendence*.

Whether or not this is the best interpretation, it has great relevance for understanding prayer. God stands beyond our reach. We cannot grasp or figure out, manipulate or control God. There are no fully adequate words. Creedal formulas and theological dissertations can never exhaust the richness of God.

Creeds and theological explanations of course have their place. In prayer, however, the most fundamental thing we do is to open the depths of our being to the transforming love of this God who dwells within us and yet is ever beyond our grasp.

In this way we grow in union with God while remaining apart. If we are willing to bear the pain of respecting God's distance, we will be able to experience the joy of God's nearness. Then in the apartness we will be united. In God's absence we will bask in God's presence. Remaining alone, we will be together.

Call to confrontation

The heart of God's revelation to Moses was the call to go to the pharaoh and see to the liberation of the enslaved Hebrew people.

The interchange that took place between God and Moses at that burning bush involved three phases. In the first phase of the dialogue it was, as always, God who took the initiative. In this prayer experience Moses did not have to inform God of the people's plight. Rather, God was already conscious of their miserable state and shared this awareness with Moses. Moses did not have to arouse concern in God by prayer. God was already deeply concerned and communicated this concern to Moses in order to enkindle in *him* greater empathy. Moses did not ask God to get involved and liberate the enslaved Hebrews. The whole dynamic of this prayer experience culminated, rather, in God's involving Moses and sending him to deliver his people from oppression.

In the second phase of this interchange Moses expressed his sense of inadequacy for this task of liberation. He asked God, *"Who am I* to go to Pharaoh and bring the sons of Israel out of Egypt?"* (Exodus 3:11, emphasis added). How could one single Hebrew confront Egypt's might and successfully challenge an institutionalized enslavement? How especially could this be done by a person who held no official position, one who was virtually unknown either to the Egyptians or to the enslaved Hebrews?

In the final phase Moses was assured of God's abiding presence: "I shall be with you" (Exodus 3:12). In the Scriptures this formula constitutes a divine assurance that God will give a person the strength necessary to carry out successfully a mission that is far beyond the individual's natural powers.

Unfortunately, from the time of Moses down through the ages and into modern times, the oppression of one people by another is a persistent human tragedy. Oppression has taken many forms. Its clearest and most dramatic expression is slavery.

Despite what we would like to think, slavery is not dead even in these modern times. Throughout many parts of the world—including this country—situations continue to exist in which people are "owned" by other people. Others have absolute power to dictate what they are to do and how they are to do it. "Ownership" is reinforced by exploitative labor policies, personal degradation, economic dependence and brutal treatment for any deviation from what "the master" says.

In some parts of the world rich people possess "house slaves"—young, uneducated, impoverished girls who work exhaustingly long hours and are deprived of any opportunity for self-betterment. In many areas of the world children are enslaved as prostitutes: imprisoned, drugged, tortured and sexually exploited by their pimps. Conditions akin to slavery continue to exist in factories and mines where employees work under unhealthy conditions, shop at company-owned stores and remain in financial bondage to their employers.

Modern oppression shows its ugly face in other ways. Institutionalized poverty deprives people of educational, cultural and economic opportunities—even of life's barest necessities. Still other people are in bondage to a spouse, parent or "friend" who lords it over them and abuses them physically and psychologically.

Where is God in all this? As in the days of Moses, God is by the side of the oppressed, seeing their miserable state, identifying with the depth of their sufferings, hearing their cries for deliverance. In our prayer God speaks of concern and compassion for the oppressed, whoever they are and wherever they be. Before we can go to inform God of their plight, God comes to us to sensitize us to their anguish and their cries. Authentic prayer puts us in touch with the God who "suffers" with the afflicted and calls us today to the ongoing work of liberation.

This challenge has different implications for different people. For some it means a call to leadership roles in confronting national dictators or oppressive employers. For others it means attacking institutionalized prejudice, the injustices perpetrated even by a democratic government, the criminal exploitation of victims by organized gangsters. Archbishop Romero and Cesar Chavez,

Martin Luther King and Father Bruce Ritter are true heirs of Moses, persons whose faith called them to such roles. For all people of faith some form of involvement awaits; God's work of freeing people from oppression continues.

Sometimes our concern for institutionalized injustice distracts us from the immediate challenge our prayer life makes on us: to confront injustice in our own individual lives. Our "pharaoh" might be an employer or a fellow worker who is bullying or harassing us or our co-workers. The pharaoh in our life might be a spouse who is treating us unjustly, a school administrator who is being unfair to a student. In our prayer, do we let God's concern send us to these pharaohs even at the cost of a job, a promotion, our reputation or some other form of vindictive retribution?

In all such instances we may, like Moses, cry out, "Who am I to go to the pharaoh?" In prayer, the answer will come: "I shall be with you." One of the fruits of prayer is the courage to confront injustice wherever we find it despite the price we may have to pay.

Conclusion

We are summoned in prayer to believe in ourselves and to allow God to call us from "within the burning bush." We come to know this God who is with us and beyond us in light of the faith of the community as well as by our own personal perception. We live out our prayer-filled response by becoming actively involved in God's compassionate concern for the victims of every kind of oppression.

Touchstones

- Does your prayer help you see in yourself the possibilities God sees in you?
- Which extreme is more tempting for you: To write off as irrelevant the community's faith experience (past and present) in favor of your private message? To limit God's communication to the past (Bible and Church Tradition) and to ignore the need to discern anew God's message for our time?
- How does your prayer respect God's distance?
- What pharaohs does your prayer call you to confront?

Chapter three

'Woe is me!'

*The word of Yahweh has meant for me
insult, derision, all day long.
I used to say, "I will not think about him,
I will not speak in his name any more."
Then there seemed to be a fire burning in my heart,
imprisoned in my bones.
The effort to restrain it wearied me,
I could not bear it.
I hear so many disparaging me,
"'Terror from every side!'
Denounce him! Let us denounce him!"*

*...But Yahweh is at my side, a mighty hero;
my opponents will stumble, mastered,
confounded by their failure;
everlasting, unforgettable disgrace will be theirs....*

*Sing to Yahweh,
praise Yahweh,
for he has delivered the soul of the needy
from the hands of evil men.*

(Jeremiah 20:8-10, 11, 13)

There is a common illusion that prayer comes easier the holier you are. We look at the saints and assume prayer wasn't difficult for them. After all, they were saints!

But the saints became saints *because* they prayed. They did not pray because they were first saints. Like us they experienced aloneness, doubts and depression in their prayer. Like us they were tempted to believe they were not being touched by God, that they were not on the right path at all.

Yet the saints prayed in darkness as well as light. In fact, they came to greater light precisely because they continued to pray despite the darkness. That's a lesson in prayer we all need to learn. And Jeremiah's prayer experience is an excellent place to start.

In 626 B.C., at the age of 20, Jeremiah had a religious experience in which he received God's call to be a prophet. It was one of the most critical periods of Israel's history: The Northern Kingdom of Israel had fallen to Assyria less than a century earlier. From 687 to 642 B.C. the Southern Kingdom, under the rule of King Manasseh, had seen a drastic moral and religious decline.

Jeremiah's prophetic ministry spanned about 40 years. It began a few years before the religious reform of King Josiah in 621 B.C.

Jeremiah stressed the covenant of love between Yahweh and Israel, and warned that dire consequences would result if the people did not abandon their idolatry and return to God. Josiah's reform brought about the kind of changes Jeremiah had preached.

But Josiah's death brought the reform to a halt, and there was a widespread return to idolatry. Under the reign of King Jehoiakim many religious and moral reforms were abandoned. Thus Jeremiah resumed his denunciation of idolatry and his call for conversion. He confronted political and religious leaders with their moral corruption.

As in the case of other prophets, Jeremiah did not meet a great deal of success. For the most part his warnings went unheeded. Political and religious leaders rejected him and plotted against him. The dire events which he predicted did in fact occur. The years of Jeremiah's ministry witnessed the Babylonian siege of Jerusalem in 597 B.C. and the final downfall of the Southern Kingdom in 587 B.C. when the Babylonians destroyed the city of Jerusalem and the Temple and carried the Jews into exile.

Glimpses of spiritual turmoil can be found in Jeremiah's prophetic writings. The dark periods of his ministry are reflected in the inner struggle and crises of faith expressed in his prayer. The prayer of Jeremiah in time of crisis contains three key elements: a complaint about his suffering; the call to conversion; trust and hope that God will carry him through the dark hour. His prayer can shed light on our own prayer in the dark moments of our spiritual journey.

Suffering and crisis in prayer

Jeremiah's prayer expressed in vivid ways the depth of his spiritual anguish:

> You have seduced me, Yahweh, and I have let
>   myself be seduced;
> you have overpowered me: you were the
>   stronger. (Jeremiah 20:7)

> Woe is me, my mother, for you have borne me
> to be a man of strife and of dissension for all the
>   land. (Jeremiah 15:10)

> Why is my suffering continual,
>   my wound incurable, refusing to be healed?
> Do you mean to be for me a deceptive stream
>   with inconstant waters? (Jeremiah 15:18)

God had called Jeremiah to a ministry that involved conflict and contention, suffering and persecution, and there seemed to be no end to the torment involved in prophesying violence and ruin as a consequence of his people's sinfulness and wrongdoing. Had God truly deceived him and abandoned him to his unhappy plight?

Once God's Word had been delight and joy to Jeremiah's heart, but now he had come to a point in his life when he wanted to abandon the prophetic mission. The depth of Jeremiah's pain is perhaps best reflected in this exclamation:

> A curse on the day when I was born,
> no blessing on the day my mother bore me!
> A curse on the man who brought my father the
>   news,
> "A son, a boy has been born to you!"
> making him overjoyed.
> May this man be like the towns
> that Yahweh overthrew without mercy;
> may he hear alarms in the morning,
> the war cry in broad daylight,
> since he did not kill me in the womb;
> my mother would have been my tomb

> Why ever did I come out of the womb
> while her womb was swollen with me.
> To live in toil and sorrow
> and to end my days in shame! (Jeremiah 20:14-18)

What would we do if a friend called at 2:00 a.m. and expressed similar sentiments?

Reflection on the crisis of faith expressed in Jeremiah's prayer can help us place our own dark moments of prayer in perspective. Doubts about God, regrets that God has entered our life and deep depression over the reality of our situation *are* compatible with the journey to holiness and to high levels of prayer. Regardless of how profound our faith and how strong our prayer life, we are never immune from the experience of God's absence. Nor are we immune from the gnawing doubt whether, after all, there is anyone on the other side of our prayer. We cannot combat these doubts with any scientific proofs that would make unnecessary our profound and humble act of faith. All we can do is to proclaim: "Lord, I believe; help my unbelief" (see Mark 9:24).

The need for conversion

Struggle though we may in the dark hours of our spiritual journey, we may occasionally lose faith in God, trust too little. We may falter in our commitment to the call God has given us. When we fail to trust, when we falter, we need conversion. We are bidden to turn our hearts more fully to God and to the call God is speaking to us. And when we do, we find a forgiving God who strengthens us in our faith and bids us to walk steadfastly in his way once again.

It seems that even Jeremiah wavered in his darkest hours, for God replied to his complaint and his questioning in these words:

> "If you come back,
> I will take you back into my service;
> and if you utter noble, not despicable, thoughts,
> you shall be as my own mouth.
> They will come back to you,
> but you must not go back to them.
> I will make you
> a bronze wall fortified against this people.
> They will fight against you
> but they will not overcome you,
> because I am with you
> to save you and to deliver you
> —it is Yahweh who speaks.
> I mean to deliver you from the hands of the wicked
> and redeem you from the clutches of the violent."
>
> (Jeremiah 15:19-21)

God's words indicate that Jeremiah needed to rededicate himself to his prophetic vocation. God invited him to conversion. God made no promise that conflict would go away or that the road would become any easier. Jeremiah was assured, however, that God would remain with him to strengthen him and deliver him from those who opposed him.

We live out our relationship with God in the entire context of our life. Our relationship with others, our call in life and our work express the same faith and love that moves us to pray. When something goes wrong in a major area of our life, it is bound to color our experience of God and to affect our prayer. At such times we may compare our depression and struggle with earlier periods in our life when we, like Jeremiah, were eager for God's Word and found delight and joy in prayer. These times afford an opportunity to rediscover God's continued assurance of supporting presence and to respond with renewed commitment.

Hope in God's abiding presence

Even in Jeremiah's darkest hours of spiritual crisis the theme of hope emerged. He was able to proclaim:

> Yahweh is at my side, a mighty hero;...
>
> Sing to Yahweh,
> praise Yahweh,
> for he has delivered the soul of the needy
> from the hands of evil men. (Jeremiah 20:11, 13)

Despite the anguish he felt and the difficulties that confronted him from all sides, Jeremiah believed that God would not abandon him. God would be with him to strengthen him. God would, in the end, enable Jeremiah to be victorious.

Conclusion

Faith in God's love and concern and the memory of God's past fidelity enable us to believe that God is present even in the most desolate hour. Pain will not be magically assuaged, nor doubts instantly dissolved. But trust in God's abiding strength can help us emerge from the darkness stronger and more faith-filled persons.

Touchstones

• Do you feel as free as Jeremiah to address your

complaint to God when doubt and despair strike?
- What dark moments of your prayer does Jeremiah's story help put in perspective?
- How is your prayer calling you to a rededication, a conversion?
- How can your prayer nourish a sense of God's abiding presence even in the darkest hour?

The prayer of Jesus

Chapter four

'Abba, Father'

"Ask, and it will be given to you; search, and you will find; knock, and the door will be opened to you. For the one who asks always receives; the one who searches always finds; the one who knocks will always have the door opened to him. Is there a man among you who would hand his son a stone when he asked for bread? Or would hand him a snake when he asked for a fish? If you, then, who are evil, know how to give your children what is good, how much more will your Father in heaven give good things to those who ask him!"
(Matthew 7:7-11)

Even when our prayer is "going well," God often seems remote and impersonal. How does God really communicate to us? How does God know and love us?

Theoretical answers to these difficulties are less than adequate. Christians depend on another answer: the person of Jesus Christ. Through Jesus and through his prayer we are able to know and love God in a new and intimate way.

Jesus, a person of prayer

The Gospel portrays Jesus as a person whose life was permeated by prayer. Jesus began his public ministry with an extraordinary religious experience at the Jordan river (Matthew 3:13-17). Thereafter he was led by the Spirit into the wilderness where he spent 40 days in solitude and fasting (Luke 4:1-3). He attended religious celebrations in the Temple (Luke 2:41; John 7:10), spent nights alone in prayer (Matthew 14:23-24), and prayed in the presence of others (Luke 22:39ff).

Besides praying in many situations, Jesus also prayed in a diversity of ways: He glorified God; he gave thanks to God for revealing truth to little ones, for food, and for raising Lazarus from the dead. He prayed for forgiveness for his enemies and asked for the preservation of his disciples from evil and for unity among his followers.

Growth in likeness to Christ demands a similar integration of authentic prayer into one's life in all its various forms: worship and praise of God's goodness; thanksgiving for the blessings that have enriched the physical, emotional and spiritual dimensions of our lives; the prayer oriented toward forgiveness and reconciliation, for without forgiveness there can be no authentic union with God; and, finally, prayer of petition.

Prayer of petition attests to our dependence on God as the ultimate source of all good. It also gives sign of our openness to God's gifts, our willingness to be more receptive to the graces and blessings that God wishes to give us, our admission that we can be transformed by God's gifts only to the degree that we desire them. Prayer of petition can strengthen our commitment to realize more fully the potential that already resides within us.

'Abba'

The one word that sums up Jesus' experience of God is *Abba*. This Aramaic word which we translate as "Father" is really an informal and intimate designation better translated as "Daddy" or "Papa."

One can only imagine the kind of intimate, personal experience of God that led Jesus to break through the categories of religious language and proclaim God *Abba*! This experience, rooted in his being one with God, could only be expressed as unity:

> "The Father and I are one." (John 10:30)

> "Do you not believe
> that I am in the Father and the Father is in me?"
> (John 14:10)

This oneness involved an intimate sharing:

> "Everything the Father has is mine." (John 16:15)

> "[Father,] all I have is yours
> and all you have is mine...." (John 17:10)

In all that he did, Jesus knew the Father was working with him:

> "I tell you most solemnly,
> the Son can do nothing by himself;
> he can do only what he sees the Father doing:
> and whatever the Father does the Son does too.

> For the Father loves the Son
> and shows him everything he does himself,
> and he will show him even greater things than these,
> works that will astonish you." (John 5:19-20)

Jesus was aware that the Father was with him, directing his life; he lived in loving response. He preached what he heard from the Father.

> "...I do nothing of myself:
> what the Father has taught me
> is what I preach." (John 8:28)

> "The words I say to you I do not speak as from myself:
> it is the Father, living in me, who is doing this work." (John 14:10)

> "My food
> is to do the will of the one who sent me,
> and to complete his work." (John 4:34)

Jesus' response to God, his *Abba*, was prayed out in the totality of his life and ministry. Thus Jesus became the fulfillment of Isaiah's prophecy:

> "Here is my servant whom I have chosen,
> my beloved, the favorite of my soul."
> (Isaiah 42:1, as quoted in Matthew 12:18)

Jesus' intimate union with the Father was expressed in the prayer he taught his disciples to pray:

> "Our Father in heaven,
> may your name be held holy,
> your kingdom come,
> your will be done,
> on earth as in heaven.
> Give us today our daily bread.
> And forgive us our debts,

as we have forgiven those who are in debt to us.
And do not put us to the test,
but save us from the evil one." (Matthew 6:9-13)

To pray as Jesus prayed

To pray as Jesus prayed means to share in Christ's experience of God as *Abba*. In order to do this, the Christian must first enter into Christ's awareness of God's intimate presence to him by prayerfully reflecting on the biblical passages that speak of Christ's unity with the Father. Through these passages, we can glimpse the inner attitude which inspired Christ's words. By reflecting on Jesus' prayer as recorded in the Gospels we can begin to contemplate the present union of the crucified and risen Christ with God, his *Abba*.

The more closely we are in touch with Christ's ongoing experience of God, the better able we are to pray as Christ challenges us to pray. To call God our *Abba* is more demanding—and hence more frightening—than we might at first suppose. In pre-Vatican II times, the liturgical formula that introduced the Lord's Prayer at the Eucharist reflected this uneasiness: "Taught by our Savior's command and formed by the Word of God, we dare to say, 'Our Father....'"

Why is it *daring*? To call God *Abba* is to own up to the intimate relationship with God to which we have been called. It is to acknowledge ourselves as daughters and sons of God. This implies our acceptance of one another as sisters and brothers.

How much easier to address God in the words more frequently used in the past,

"Almighty and Eternal God"! That puts God at a safe distance. We can honor such a God by accepting our createdness, by offering worship and sacrifice and by obeying God's laws and commands—as we conveniently understand them.

Once we pray with Christ, "*Abba*, Father," we commit ourselves to respond to God's intimate, unlimited love. Such response knows no bounds save death and resurrection.

This perception of God as our *Abba* can gradually lead us to an awareness that infinite Love dwells within us. It can help us deepen our conviction that God speaks to us and works with us in the context of our own personal history. Then we can meet God in our lives, in our work, in our family and friends. If we can not find God there, what is the use of looking anywhere else?

Conclusion

Our prayer is our response to the God we call *Abba*. We respond by accepting God's love and by saying yes to the divine call to filial relationship. We pray by listening to God speaking through our lives and by attuning ourselves to the works God is striving to do in and through us.

Such filial prayer does not take place only in quiet moments of solitude or in the exercise of formal prayer. It happens in a concrete way every time our yes to life, to others, to the way we work is guided and permeated by our belief that God is *Abba* of us all.

Touchstones

- Jesus was a "person of prayer." Are you?
- Does your prayer life, like Jesus', include a diversity of prayer forms: of praise, thanksgiving and reconciliation as well as petition?
- Do you allow God to come close enough in your prayer to be addressed as *Abba*?
- Do you experience this intimacy with God, the *Abba*, as "daring"?

Chapter five

'The Word was made flesh'

In the beginning was the Word;
the Word was with God
and the Word was God....

The Word was made flesh,
he lived among us,
and we saw his glory,
the glory that is his as the only Son of the Father,
full of grace and truth. (John 1:1, 14)

A rather common assumption is that in order to pray, one has to move as far away as possible from involvement with the "flesh" and the world. This "dualism" is part of our Greek philosophical heritage and sees body and soul, flesh and spirit, world and God as separate and opposing realities.

The Incarnation of Jesus Christ challenges this dualistic view. In Jesus the Word of God became flesh. The Word of God moved into the very center of human existence. Human existence itself became the new focal point of God's encounter with the human race.

In this chapter we consider four important aspects of the Incarnation that have particular relevance for contemporary prayer and spirituality.

In our humanity

First: In the enfleshment of Jesus Christ, God has come to us in a most human way. Hence we meet God *here* on the human scene. We need not search for God in the sky or in the heavens. We need not deny our humanness, our bodiliness, to find God. We need not flee into the desert. What we have to do is open our eyes to our own humanity.

For the Word of God has become one of us, identified with our human limitations and our human mortality. Through death Christ has passed into new bodily risen life. Having conquered death, Christ is totally with the Father and with us, forever a human being among human beings.

We find God, then, through our humanity. Our response to God involves responding to our humanity. We become more God-like by becoming more fully human. We discover what it means to be fully human by contemplating the Word in human flesh.

In the New Testament, Jesus Christ replaces the Temple; the new dwelling place of God is in the crucified and risen body of Christ. Christ dwells with us, giving us his Spirit so that we may become one body in him. Christian prayer is saying yes to becoming this one body.

Present in love

Second: The enfleshment of the Word is the sign and sacrament of God's personal involvement with humans.

> Yes, God loved the world so much
> that he gave his only Son….(John 3:16)

> God's love for us was revealed
> when God sent into the world his only Son
> so that we could have life through him;
> this is the love I mean:
> not our love for God,
> but God's love for us when he sent his Son
> to be the sacrifice that takes our sins away.
> (1 John 4:9-10)

This love, revealed in the Incarnation, manifests God's initiative and God's concern for human well-being. It also speaks of the divine forgiveness and of an infinite desire for human reconciliation. It gives evidence that from the beginning humans were created for the greatest possible union with God in and through Jesus Christ. God made humanity in such a way that one day Creator and creatures could come together in the fullest way possible: in the very enfleshment of God's Word.

Christian prayer involves believing in the intimacy of God's love. It is being open to God's involvement in our history. It is saying yes to the union toward which God draws us, saying amen to the wedding of divinity and humanity.

Within human limits

Third: In the Incarnation the Word of God accepted the human condition. In taking our flesh,

Jesus assumed the characteristics and limitations inherent to our state. He had to grow as humans grow: slowly and at times painfully. He had to live and work with limited knowledge and limited physical, psychic and emotional energy. He had to face the realities of his sexuality. He had to take time to eat, drink and sleep. He had to accept the fact that he was not Superman, that he was better at some endeavors than at others, and that he did not possess every possible human talent.

Enfleshment also means accepting historical limits: living in time and in a specific set of circumstances. Jesus was born into a particular Jewish family and lived in Palestine during the first third of the first century. He could only relate to his world within current Jewish thought patterns and set against the historical context of his people's religion. He was, like all humans, shaped by his culture.

The prayer life of Jesus involved acceptance of his specific human situation. He said yes to his Father in terms of the concrete realities that constituted his earthly situation. He became all he was able to be as a human being. He had to make the best of what he could not change even as he worked for the transformation of the human situation.

Our prayer is human prayer. Hence our yes to God necessarily involves a yes to ourselves and to our basic human condition. Accepting our human createdness involves a delicate balance of two realities: being comfortable with the limitations we cannot change and, at the same time, striving to actualize all our potential for growth and development. Both of these challenges can be difficult for us to meet.

Accepting the built-in limitations of the human condition does not come easily. Many of us possess the super-person urge. We would like to be the best singer, the best athlete, the best student, the best spouse, the best parent, the best in our profession. Yet we keep discovering we are only human. We are imperfect and limited in all we do.

We might wish we did not have to "waste" so much time sleeping, eating and tending to the basic necessities of survival. We regret getting old. We are uneasy about our sexuality. We resent our mortality.

We often express discomfort at being associated with the human race: "There is so much man-made evil in the world." "So many human policies are utterly stupid." "There is so much greed and insensitivity." Even our ethnic background can be an embarrassment—especially if we study much history! Sometimes we may want to keep some of our relatives hidden in a distant closet. As one close friend used to wonder: "What did Christ ever see in the human race to bother dying for it?"

Yet the Incarnation inspires us to believe it is "divine" to be human. God has so accepted the human condition that the Word has taken on human flesh. Christian prayer must involve no less.

At the heart of Christian prayer is the acceptance of our human identity. We respond to God in prayer by being authentically human.

Hence all of the things we do for human survival and for human growth and development are our yes to what God wishes for us.

In the ordinary

Finally: God communicates to us in the ordinary circumstances of our life. We are touched by God not only in formal moments of prayer when we are alone in our "desert." God is also present in our work and play, our sorrows and joys, our failures and successes, our eating, drinking and sleeping. God is present to us in one another: our friends and our enemies, the poor and the wealthy, the happy, the desolate and the sick. To pray is to discover God in the ordinary. To pray is to respond to God's presence by being present to each other, to be fully alive to the diverse moments that mark the rhythm of human life.

Conclusion

The Incarnation radically restructures human prayer. Christians cannot view the world and the flesh as inherently evil for the Word of God has chosen it for a dwelling place. We encounter our God in the ordinariness, the limitations, the humanness of our lives.

Touchstones

- Do you say yes in prayer to your humanness—to your body, your limits, your mortality, your world?
- Does your prayer express belief in the intimacy of God's love for you?

- How does your prayer help to balance the human limits you cannot change against your Christian call to transform the human situation?
- Does your prayer attend the presence of God in the people and events of your everyday life?

Chapter six

'By their fruits...'

*"You did not choose me,
no, I chose you;
and I commissioned you
to go out and bear fruit,
fruit that will last;
and then the Father will give you
anything you ask him in my name.
What I command you
is to love one another." (John 15:16-17)*

We often treat prayer and action as if they were mutually opposed. We identify prayer with an hour on Sunday or with those formal moments of prayer in which we shut out all else. Then we become so wrapped up in activity that we complain of having no time to pray.

Instead of this dichotomy, prayer and action ought to touch each other. In prayer we consecrate and dedicate to God all we are and all we do. In our activity we allow the insights and deepened relationship with God gained in prayer to guide our decisions, to permeate our style of action and to enrich the quality of our relationships with the people for whom and with whom we work. Prayer, as our response to God, can never be merely verbal. It must be lived out if we are truly to respond to God's call for us:

> "It is not those who say to me, 'Lord, Lord,' who will enter the kingdom of heaven, but the person who does the will of my Father in heaven."
>
> (Matthew 7:21)

This intimate connection between prayer and action is exemplified in the Gospel portrait of Jesus. Christ's prayer was vividly expressed in the way he lived and in the way he related to others. In this chapter we will consider three aspects of the spirituality with which Christ lived out his prayer life in action.

Christian anger

A colleague and friend once surprised some of his listeners by exhorting them to "Christian anger." They were startled because, like most of us, they had been trained to perceive anger as a vice inconsistent with the "meek and mild" ideal falsely identified with the "Christian spirit."

Webster defines anger as "a strong passion or emotion of displeasure, and usually antagonism, excited by a sense of injury or insult" and goes on to define antagonism as "active opposition or resistance." Anger thus defined is morally indifferent. What makes it right or wrong is the reason *why* one is angry and *how* one expresses it. To express anger out of hatred for another is obviously in conflict with Christian love. But to be indifferent, unmoved by the plight of others, is equally unchristian.

Christian prayer, because it leads to greater love and compassion for fellow humans, makes us more sensitive to what happens to others and heightens our sense of what is just and decent. Consequently, it often leads to impatience—even outrage.

The Gospel provides a powerful example of Christian anger. When Jesus went up to the Temple, he found people selling sheep and pigeons and saw the money changers sitting at their counters. He made a cord whip and drove them all out of the Temple along with the animals. He went further: He scattered the money changers' coins and knocked over their tables. Then he gave orders to the pigeon sellers:

> "'Take all of this out of here and stop turning my Father's house into a market.' Then his disciples remembered the words of Scripture: 'Zeal for your house will devour me.'" (John 2:16-17)

Confronted with this scene, we might prefer to explain it away as the work of the evangelist's imagination with no bearing on the "real" Jesus. Or we might admit that it happened but doubt that Jesus really was angry as we know anger. His heartbeat did not speed up; no blood rushed to his head; he never raised his voice; each motion was measured with precision.

But if we put ourselves inside that scene, we cannot accept that antiseptic view. No one drives merchants out of a public place—especially if they have paid to be there—by polite requests. Nor is it that easy to get rid of a number of cattle and sheep. While Jesus' action did not go unchallenged, he was able to command compliance—perhaps the most remarkable aspect of the story. After all, Jesus was clearly outnumbered, and it is hard to believe that all the Temple police were out to lunch at the same time. Imagine a similar scene taking place today in St. Peter's Square or St. Patrick's Cathedral!

To those inclined to say the Temple scene was the one isolated incident in which Jesus showed anger, I recommend the careful reading of Jesus' sevenfold indictment of the scribes and Pharisees recorded in Matthew 23:13-32. Again, one has to try to get inside that scene and imagine Jesus' voice and body language to sense the outrage that provoked that speech.

Of course prayer can help us control unchristian expression of anger. But it must also help us *get* angry—sometimes really angry—over those things that demand outrage in light of the Gospel command to love one another as Christ loves us (see John 15:12). Where is our prayer life if we can, for example, blithely turn the other way when a fellow worker is being unfairly treated on the job, or if we can remain indifferent to the organized sexual exploitation of children or to the unjust practices of the slum landlord?

Evangelical poverty

Gospel poverty has nothing to do with destitution. Destitution is an evil to be conquered, not a virtue to be cultivated. Neither does evangelical poverty have anything to do with a dualism that despises material things and longs for a spiritual state of disembodiment.

Christianity, after all, is rooted in the Genesis insight: "God looked at everything he had made, and he found it very good" (Genesis 1:31, NAB).

Evangelical poverty is the attitude toward material things practiced and preached by Christ. It places values in proper perspective so that we allow our love of God and others to regulate our pursuit and use of material things.

Evangelical poverty is rooted in the belief that God is the ultimate creator of all reality, that the purpose of creation is to bring us to new union with God and with one another in Jesus Christ, that the ultimate dominion over the earth belongs to God, not to humans. From these beliefs flow three specific challenges to our life and our prayer:

1) *To trust*. Christ challenges us not to be anxious about material necessities, but to trust in the provident love of God.

> "That is why I am telling you not to worry about your life and what you are to eat, nor about your body and how you are to clothe it. Surely life means more than food, and the body more than clothing! Look at the birds in the sky. They do not sow or reap or gather into barns; yet your heavenly Father feeds them. Are you not worth much more than they are? Can any of you, for all his worrying, add one single cubit to his span of life? And why worry about clothing? Think of the flowers growing in the fields; they never have to work or spin; yet I assure you that not even Solomon in all his regalia was robed like one of these. Now if that is how God clothes the grass in the field which is there today and thrown into the furnace tomorrow, will he not much more look after you, you men of little faith? So do not worry; do not say, 'What are we to eat? What are we to

drink? How are we to be clothed?' It is the pagans who set their hearts on all these things. Your heavenly Father knows you need them all. Set your hearts on his kingdom first, and on his righteousness, and all these other things will be given you as well. So do not worry about tomorrow: tomorrow will take care of itself. Each day has enough trouble of its own."

(Matthew 6:25-34)

If we have this trust, we can put aside our fears of the future and relax and enjoy the present. The rat race gives way to more tranquil living. Hoarding gives way to sharing. People become more important than things.

2) *To put people first*. Jesus' love and involvement with people inspired his use of things. He had no place to lay his head (Luke 9:58) so he could be free and available to minister to the needs of others. He did not take time to eat when another person needed him (John 4:31-35). Yet he was present at a wedding feast (John 2:1-10) and attended parties with sinners who needed his healing presence (Mark 2:15-17).

Detachment from things is not in itself a virtue. Concerned involvement with others is. If people come first in our life, being present to them in understanding and love will take priority over the accumulation of material goods.

3) *To be stewards of the earth*. Christian poverty acknowledges that ultimately we are not the owners of the earth. It belongs to God. The earth is entrusted to our care for the short while that we are pilgrims on this planet. We are stewards, called by God to care for the earth out of concern for one another. We are accountable for our

stewardship. There is no justification for raping the land, poisoning the waters, preparing for nuclear holocaust. There is no justification for political and economic structures that systematically prevent food and other necessities from reaching millions of members of the human family. We are held responsible for using our minds, imaginations and hearts to find ways of sharing with all a fair portion of the earth's God-given abundance.

Christian prayer is nothing if it does not bring us into deeper awareness of God as the *Abba* of us all and make us more conscious of our radical sisterhood and brotherhood. It is empty if it does not inspire us to regard and use the things of the earth in a way that gives sign of—sacramentalizes— God's love and generous compassion and our respect for the earth's real owner.

Love of enemies

Christ did not invent the mandate to love. That command was enunciated centuries earlier in the Hebrew Scriptures. The extraordinary dimension Jesus introduced was the challenge to love the *enemy*.

> "You have learned how it was said: You must love your neighbor and hate your enemy. But I say this to you: love your enemies and pray for those who persecute you; in this way you will be sons of your Father in heaven, for he causes his sun to rise on bad men as well as good, and his rain to fall on honest and dishonest men alike. For if you love those who love you, what right have you to claim any credit? Even the tax collectors do as much, do they not? And if you save your greetings for your

brothers, are you doing anything exceptional? Even the pagans do as much, do they not? You must therefore be perfect just as your heavenly Father is perfect." (Matthew 5:43-48)

Jesus' manifestation of love for the enemy included four elements:

1) Jesus loved the enemy enough to confront them. He had the courage to tell them where he thought they were wrong and why he disagreed with them. He could call people hypocrites to their faces. When he did so, it was not to destroy but to bring forth truth and afford an opportunity for conversion.

Too often we may be inclined to pretend we have no enemies. We dare not confront another person "eyeball to eyeball," but prefer either to sweep our differences under the proverbial rug or to suppress our hostile feelings until the person is beyond earshot. Before we can love our enemies we must admit we have them.

2) Jesus did not solve the problem of enemies by trying to obliterate them. He rejected his followers' plea to call down "fire from heaven" on an inhospitable Samaritan village (see Luke 9: 54-56). When his enemies finally seized him, he ordered Peter to put away his sword (see John 18:11). Christ knew that hatred and retaliation only intensify hostility and create more enemies. Love alone has the power to do away with enmity.

Prayer must lead us to evaluate how we, as individuals and as a society, approach our enemies today. How do we treat those who have harmed us? How do we protect ourselves against those whom we fear? To put it concretely, we must face the question of how much we are allowing authentic Christian prayer to influence our attitudes and actions on issues like capital punishment, gun control, the American penal system and the nuclear arms race.

3) Christ prayed for his enemies and forgave them (see Matthew 5:44; Luke 23:34). To pray for an enemy is to show concern for that person's well-being. It gives evidence of *willingness* to love, even if all we *feel* is anger and intense dislike. Praying for an enemy implies forgiveness, even if wounds and scars continue to be painful reminders. One thing is certain: It is impossible to continue for long both hating and praying for an enemy. Either we will surrender the hatred or abandon the prayer.

4) Jesus reached out to those defined as "enemy" by the establishment of his day: the leper, the Samaritan, the tax collector, the sinner (see Mark 1:40-45; John 4:1-42; Matthew 9:10-13). Prayer must give us the enlightenment and the courage to reach out and touch today's outcasts: the ex-convict, the seriously handicapped, the homosexual, the emotionally disturbed.

This outreach must not be limited to personal contact and the setting aside of our individual prejudices. It must also include the effort to change those societal structures that deny access to jobs, neighborhood housing and educational and recreational opportunities.

Conclusion

Christian anger, evangelical poverty, love of enemies—these manifestations of prayer in action present a radical challenge to the values of the world. The more closely our prayer and our actions are intertwined, the more our lives, like Christ's, make the Kingdom visible wherever we go.

Touchstones
- Does your prayer help you *get* angry over those things that demand outrage in light of the gospel?
- Does your prayer challenge you to the freedom and the responsibility of poverty in the gospel sense?
- What place do your enemies have in your prayer?

Chapter seven

'Like a grain of wheat'

..."*Now the hour has come
for the Son of Man to be glorified.
I tell you, most solemnly,
unless a wheat grain falls on the ground and dies,
it remains only a single grain;
but if it dies,
it yields a rich harvest.
Anyone who loves his life loses it;
anyone who hates his life in this world
will keep it for the eternal life.
If a man serves me, he must follow me,
wherever I am, my servant will be there too.
If anyone serves me, my Father will honor him.
Now my soul is troubled.
What shall I say:
Father, save me from this hour?
But it was for this very reason that I have come to
 this hour.
Father, glorify your name!"*

*A voice came from heaven, "I have glorified it,
and I will glorify it again." (John 12:23-28)*

Death is a reality we like to push to the periphery of our consciousness: Now we live, *tomorrow* we die. We pray it will come later in our journey rather than too early. And when the hour does come, we pray God will give us the grace we need for a "peaceful and happy" death.

Death, however, is an integral part of life. From the first moment of our existence, we carry within us the seeds of our own mortality. We are, from the beginning, oriented toward death. The final death to which all earthly life leads is itself the culmination of the countless dyings and risings that comprise our growth in life.

Prayer, then, must have a much deeper relationship to death than merely seeking help for life's final moment. In prayer we face the realities of our life and we offer our decision to become the kind of person God is calling us to be. We say yes to the fuller life God wants for us—to the losses, the good-byes, the daily dyings that growth necessitates. We say yes to the challenges of making our home, our work environment and society itself a better place to live regardless of the difficulties, the rejection, the dyings that might result from our commitment.

An essential element of Christ's prayer is the offering of himself to the mission the Father has given him and accepting the personal consequences of that dedication even unto death on a cross. This willingness of Jesus to do God's work even at the price of his death is brought out in parallel ways in the Gospels of Luke and John. Luke describes much of Jesus' ministry as taking place on a freely chosen journey to Jerusalem, where Jesus meets his death. In the fourth Gospel, John centers the ministry of Jesus around the "hour of glory," that hour on Good Friday when Jesus freely gives up his life.

In this chapter we probe the connection between Christ's prayer life and his ministry which embraced death and resurrection. In light of this consideration, we explore the paschal dimension in all Christian prayer.

Prayer and ministry

Christ's prayer and his ministry were intimately linked. His prayer life expressed itself in ministering to the spiritual and personal needs of people. His ministry was inspired and directed by his prayer life.

Christ's public ministry began with a religious experience during his baptism at the Jordan: the sight of the Spirit descending like a dove and a voice from heaven approving Jesus and his mission (see Matthew 3:16-17).

Afterwards the Spirit led Jesus into the wilderness (see Matthew 4:1-11). For 40 days Jesus rejected the temptations to pursue any course that would contradict the mission his Father had given him to perform. He would not allow his ministry to become merely a magical means of providing physical bread because the bread he was sent to give was God's life-giving Word. He refused to attract a large following by doing the spectacular because faith can never be formed merely on the basis of signs, however extraordinary. He rejected the path of political revolution because the salvation that Jesus came to bring cannot be achieved solely by uprooting political structures, but only by the conversion and transformation of the human heart.

Christ's mission was to proclaim the Kingdom of God. This Kingdom is built on truth and love, justice, peace and holiness. Christ preached God as his *Abba* and invited people to share in this relationship. He called people to a new unity of love that would allow no prejudice and know no outcasts. He showed that personal commitment to God and to one another could not be prescribed by mere laws; the challenge of discipleship goes far beyond what can be contained in any code.

Because of his pursuit of this mission, Christ began to meet rejection. Some saw him as a blasphemer (see Luke 5:21). Others were upset that he ate with sinners (see Mark 2:16). Still others were incensed by his violations of the Sabbath (see Matthew 12:9-14; Mark 2:23-28; Luke 13:10-17). His enemies became ever more determined to put him to death (see John 11:53). But Jesus stayed faithful to the work God had given him to do. He accepted the suffering and death that would be the inevitable consequence of his ministry (see Matthew 16:21-23 and 17:22-23; Luke 9:44-45; John 12:20-28).

Faith and prayer without good works are empty (see James 2:14-17). Prayer must lead us to minister to the needs of others. Our ministry must also be filled with prayer. True contemplation expresses itself in active ministering. Redemptive ministering needs to be contemplative.

Prayer enables us to participate in the ongoing redemptive work of Christ by ministering as he ministers. Like Christ, we must resist temptations opposed to authentic Christian ministry. While our ministering includes providing material necessities, it can never be reduced to that. Addressing the physical needs of others must be a sign of more lasting bread: the Word and the gift of self in the name of Christ. The value of Christian ministry cannot be measured by spectacular signs (the size of the crowd at our church services, the amount of publicity our efforts attract). Finally, while there is necessarily a political dimension to being human and while we are called to address ourselves to the political society in which we live, redemption can never be achieved by politics alone.

We must pray in order to become imbued with the truth and love, the justice, peace and holiness of Christ. Then our ministering will display the qualities that manifest the reign of God and transform the human condition.

Our ministering involves sacrifice. To share in the work of Christ is to share in his cross, as Jesus warned his disciples (see Matthew 10:17-25). When we reach out in love to another, we risk being rejected. When we stand up for the truth, we risk ridicule. When we speak out for justice and respect for human rights, we risk being treated unjustly and further denied our own rights.

The prayer of one who ministers to others involves dedicating one's energies and embracing an often inevitable portion of the cross.

> "What shall I say: Father, save me from this hour?
> But it was for this very reason that I have come to this hour.
> Father, glorify your name!" (John 12:27-28)

The Last Supper

The Last Supper was a celebration of the Passover meal. Jesus, rooted in his Jewish heritage, commemorated the saving event whereby the Israelite people were delivered from slavery in Egypt and led to the Promised Land. Gathered with his disciples around a supper table, Jesus took the Passover bread and wine and gave it new meaning. He made this ritual gesture a sign of his freely accepted death for the liberation and redemption of all humanity.

Even at the very end, faced with the crucifixion, Jesus remained faithful to his ministry. He did not back away from what he had proclaimed in his words and in his works. In expressing ritually his embrace of the cross as an inevitable consequence of his course, Jesus affirmed and ratified all he had done on behalf of humankind during the period of his public ministry.

In John's version of the Last Supper, Jesus employed another gesture to symbolize his acceptance of death: He washed the feet of his disciples. This was an action even Jewish slaves could not be required to perform. In this action Jesus openly accepted his role as the Servant of Yahweh who suffers for the redemption of the people and thus enters into his glory (see Isaiah 52:13—53:12).

The Last Supper offers two insights significant for contemporary prayer. First, it is important to celebrate in a ritual way our dedication to the call to minister to others. The Christian does this in a solemn way in the Eucharist. This ritual offering is authentic and valuable to the degree that we are committed to our particular vocation. The communal celebration of this commitment can, in turn, affirm and strengthen our ongoing dedication.

Second, ordinary things in our life like food and drink can sacramentalize—visibly signify—the presence of Christ and our response. While this is done in a special way in the Eucharist, all our meals can have a prayer dimension. Food and drink can also be used effectively in other group prayer situations.

Unto death on a cross

In order to appreciate Christ's prayer as his hour became imminent, it is important to keep in mind the human dimensions of Christ's death. Christ loved life; he was sensitive to its beauty and its possibilites. He also loved people and had built some intimate human relationships. As for us, death meant for Christ the surrender of his human life and his earthly relationships as he had experienced them. For Christ death also meant, as it does for us, a plunge into the unknown. Before Good Friday Christ had no human experience of death, only the conviction and trust that there would be life on the other side and that he would be with God. What this would mean in human terms was unknown to him. In this context we can understand Christ's anguish as he prayed in the garden of Gethsemane.

From the cross Christ cried out, "'*Eli, Eli, lama sabachthani*?' that is, 'My God, my God, why have you deserted me?'" (Matthew 27:46). To understand what these words really mean we must recall that they are the opening verse of Psalm 22. This lament begins with the kind of question that humans down through the ages have asked when confronted with suffering. The Psalm then answers its own question:

> In you our fathers trusted;
>   they trusted, and you delivered them.
>   (Psalm 22:5, NAB)

The Psalm ends with this proclamation:

> I will proclaim your name to my brethren;
>   in the midst of the assembly I will praise you:
> "You who fear the LORD, praise him;
>   all you descendants of Jacob, give glory to him;
>   revere him, all you descendants of Israel!
> For he has not spurned nor disdained the
>   wretched man in his misery,
> Nor did he turn his face away from him,
>   but when he cried out to him, he heard him."
> So by your gift will I utter praise in the vast
>   assembly;
>   I will fulfill my vows before those who fear
>   him.
> The lowly shall eat their fill;
>   they who seek the LORD shall praise him:
>   "May your hearts be ever merry!"
>
> All the ends of the earth
>   shall remember and turn to the LORD;
> All the families of the nations
>   shall bow down before him.
> For the dominion is the LORD's

> and he rules the nations.
> To him alone shall bow down
> > all who sleep in the earth;
> Before him shall bend
> > all who go down into the dust.
> And to him my soul shall live;
> > my descendants shall serve him.
> Let the coming generation be told of the LORD
> > that they may proclaim to a people yet to be
> > > born the justice he has shown.
>
> > (Psalm 22:23-32, NAB)

In Luke's Gospel, Jesus' last words echo the psalmist's prayer of trust:

> "Father, into your hands I commit my spirit."
> (Luke 23:46)

One of the greatest obstacles to believing in and praying to a loving God is suffering and death, especially when this is unjustly inflicted on the innocent. We ask where God was when six million Jews and six million Gentiles were exterminated by the Nazis in the holocaust. Where was God when a four-year-old was brutally raped and murdered? Where is God when innocent children are killed in Northern Ireland and in the Middle East?

For the Christian there is no theoretical answer to the problem. There is only a practical answer: the same place where God was when Jesus was crucified. The prayer of Jesus clearly indicates his belief that God, his *Abba*, was with him and would be with him on the other side of death. Where was God on Good Friday? God was with Jesus, "suffering" with him as co-victim of the human evil and hostility that crucified him. God was there—not to take Jesus magically down from the cross, but to raise him up.

Where is God when we suffer evil and tragedy? God is with us, "suffering" with us in compassionate love. God is there, present to us, enabling us to find resurrection in our own dying.

Christian prayer inspires us to do all we can to avoid and conquer evil. It also enables us to accept in faith and trust the suffering and evil we cannot avoid. Christian prayer makes it possible for us to perceive a loving, compassionate and redeeming God in the very depths of our own sorrow, an *Abba* whose hands wait to receive us.

The prayer of the risen Christ

Christ passed through death into risen life in order to be forever with us. Now he prays for us and gives us his Spirit. Luke's Gospel depicts Christ at the table on Easter Sunday with two disciples to whom he had earlier been explaining the Scriptures. Christ "took the bread and said the blessing; then he broke it and handed it to them" (Luke 24:30). Only then did they recognize him, but he vanished from their sight.

In John's Gospel Christ appeared to the disciples gathered in a room and greeted them with,

> "Peace be with you.
> As the Father sent me,
> so am I sending you."

After saying this he breathed on them and said:

> "Receive the Holy Spirit.
> For those whose sins you forgive,
> they are forgiven;

for those whose sins you retain,
they are retained." (John 20:21-23)

Luke's Gospel ends with the Ascension scene:

"Then he took them out as far as the outskirts of Bethany, and lifting up his hands he blessed them. Now as he blessed them, he withdrew from them and was carried up to heaven. They worshiped him and then went back to Jerusalem full of joy; and they were continually in the Temple praising God." (Luke 24:50-53)

This Christ who is with the Father continues to be with us "...always; yes, to the end of time" (Matthew 28:20).

The Resurrection narratives give us perception into the ongoing prayer life of Christ and his continued Spirit-filled involvement with us. This prayer and Spirit-giving action is visibly expressed in the sacramental life of the Christian community. Christ is present through Baptism and Confirmation, giving the gift of the Spirit who enables us to relate to God as Father. He is present in the Sacraments of Reconciliation and Anointing of the Sick, communicating forgiveness and healing. He is present in the Eucharist, giving the gift of himself in bread and wine.

Christian prayer has a sacramental dimension. As a baptized people we live our lives in increased openness to the risen Christ's life-giving Spirit. We are receptive to Christ's forgiveness and healing and, in turn, share in forgiving and healing others. As a Eucharistic community we enter more deeply into communion with Christ in order to become more fully his body, his people, for the life of the world.

Conclusion

Christian prayer, like Christian life, is immersed in the death and resurrection of Christ. From the moment of our Baptism our lives are laid down so that his life may fill us. In our prayer we look for strength for our commitment; in our celebration of the sacraments we tap the power of the risen Christ and are formed with our brothers and sisters into his very body.

Touchstones

- In your prayer, do you wrestle with the temptations which oppose ministering in a truly Christlike way?
- To what extent does your participation in Eucharist reflect the strength of your Christian commitment?
- In your prayer, do you look to the cross for comfort in your own suffering?
- Does your experience of the sacramental life bind you more closely to the Christian community, the body of the risen Lord?

Chapter eight

'Teach us to pray'

"In your prayers do not babble as the pagans do, for they think that by using many words will make themselves heard. Do not be like them; your Father knows what you need before you ask him. So you should pray like this:

"Our Father in heaven...." (Matthew 6:7-9)

Could it be that prayer is really much easier than we think? Perhaps we are the ones who complicate it by convincing ourselves that we are not prayerful people unless we go through many gyrations and spend long hours performing complex spiritual exercises.

The hallmark of the prayer Christ explicitly taught is simplicity. Jesus took out the complications and put prayer within the reach of the ordinary person. In this chapter we examine four aspects of that simplicity: a simple form of address ("Father"), a simple attitude (seeking refreshment), a simple place for prayer (everywhere), a simple style (unbound by formulas).

'Father'

Jesus taught us to address God with the simple, familiar term *Father*. Jesus taught no list of complicated titles for speaking of God, no lengthy, complex formulas of prayer. He gave no abstract, speculative treatises on God or on the art of communicating with God. He simply told us to pray, "Our Father, who art in heaven."

Could Christ have made it any simpler? We all learned early to run to a parent with our needs. Most of us have rather happy memories of our fathers and mothers. Those whose experiences have not been good are at least aware of fathers and mothers who are good and loving people.

Christ taught us to think of God and to relate to God in the light of the first and basic human relationship, the relationship of a daughter or son to a parent. Christ thus reduced the psychological distance between transcendent God and finite human that can make prayer so formidable. Speaking from his own intimacy with God, Jesus invited us to call *his* Father *our* Father.

Refreshment

Christ taught us to approach prayer as something that refreshes and gives rest.

> "Come to me all you who labor and are overburdened, and I will give you rest. Shoulder my yoke and learn from me, for I am gentle and humble in heart, and you will find rest for your souls. Yes, my yoke is easy and my burden light."
> (Matthew 11:28-30)

The prayer to which Christ invites us is gift and grace, not a new legalism. Christ intends prayer to bring us peace and strength, not add a stressful burden.

Do we approach prayer primarily in terms of fulfilling our "spiritual duties"? Do we fear that unless we pray "properly" we will fail to curry God's favor? Do we struggle so hard at prayer that it becomes another exhausting task on top of all the day's other burdens?

Our American cultural upbringing often keeps us from feeling good about ourselves or feeling we are acomplishing anything unless we are working hard. Hence we may tend to make prayer an ordeal. But Christ bids us to pray in such a way as to find rest in him. Prayer can bring us rest, peace and joy if we learn to relax and taste the gentleness of Christ. The experience of such gentleness can indeed refresh us and enable us to be a source of refreshment to a strained and stressful world.

'In spirit and truth'

One of the issues that fueled hostility between Jews and Samaritans was a dispute over the place of true worship. The Samaritans worshiped on Mount Gerizim, while the Jews claimed that the Jerusalem Temple was the place for authentic worship.

When a Samaritan woman confronted Jesus with this dispute, he refused to attach importance to either site.

> "Believe me, woman, the hour is coming
> when you will worship the Father neither on this
>   mountain nor in Jerusalem.
> …God is spirit,

And those who worship
must worship in spirit and truth." (John 4:21, 24)

Prayer then, is not tied down to a place. **We pray wherever we are by being open to the Spirit of truth and love who communicates to us in the innermost depths of our being**. By the power of this Spirit we are led to the complete truth (see John 16:13). By the power of this Spirit we pray to the Father of Jesus Christ.

Free from formulas

We need not clutter our prayers with multiplicity of words:

> "In your prayers do not babble as the pagans do, for they think that by using many words they will make themselves heard." (Matthew 6:7)

There comes to mind the complaint a quite religious person once made. "I am so busy trying to get through my prayers," she said, "that I have no time left to pray." Christ's invitation is to let go of the *prayers* so that we might *pray*. Prayers are for our benefit, not God's. When prayers stand in the way of really praying, we must opt for the latter. God desires a prayerful heart, not prayers.

A life of prayer tends to simplify. At an early stage lengthy prayers, wordy formulas and meditations crammed with thoughts feed our prayer life. Later we find that words and thoughts stand in the way. We pray in fewer words and spend more time in silent communion with God. If we feel guilty about abandoning formulas that served us in the past, we can rest confident in Christ's call to cease "babbling" and let the Spirit lead us to communication with God.

Conclusion

The simplicity in prayer Jesus taught will lead us to a deeper and more authentic union with God. The union toward which Christian prayer is oriented is described in the parable of the vine and the branches (see John 15:1-17). Christ is the true vine; the Father is the vinedresser; we are the branches. Christ challenges us:

> "Make your home in me, as I make mine in you ...Whoever remains in me, with me in him, bears fruit in plenty...." (John 15:4, 5)

Touchstones

- Is your prayer moving in the direction of the simplicity Jesus taught?
- In your prayer, do you find the refreshment Jesus promised?
- How can you further free your prayer from wearying complications?

The prayer of disciples: Paul and Mary

Chapter nine

'Through him, with him, in him'

The fact is, brothers, and I want you to realize this, the Good News I preached is not a human message that I was given by men, it is something I learned only through a revelation of Jesus Christ. You must have heard of my career as a practicing Jew, how merciless I was in persecuting the Church of God, how much damage I did to it, how I stood out among other Jews of my generation, and how enthusiastic I was for the traditions of my ancestors.

Then God, who had specially chosen me while I was still in my mother's womb, called me through his grace and chose to reveal his Son in me, so that I might preach the Good News about him to the pagans. I did not stop to discuss this with any human being. Nor did I go up to Jerusalem to see those who were already apostles before me, but I went off to Arabia at once and later went straight back from there to Damascus. Even when after three years I went up to Jerusalem to visit Cephas and stayed with him for fifteen days, I did not see any of the other apostles; I only saw James, the brother of the Lord, and I swear before God that what I have just written is the literal truth.

(Galatians 1:11-20)

John's Gospel describes the first sign that Jesus performed during his public ministry: changing six huge jars of water into wine (see John 2:1-12). The water Christ used had been set in place for a designated purpose, the purification rites prescribed by the Mosaic law. Hence, the water symbolized the old dispensation. When the prophets described the messianic era they spoke of an abundance of wine (see Isaiah 25:6, Joel 4:18) as a symbol of the fullness of messianic blessings. Christ's changing of water into an abundance of fine wine is a sign for those of faith that he is indeed the One who brings the fullness of God's graces and blessings.

Too often Christians have turned back to the water of the purification rites rather than drink of the new wine. Too often we have prayed in the light of philosophical notions and pre-Christian conceptions, missing the insight that Christ radically changed our approach to God. Christian prayer must be rooted in Christ and in his prayer so that, through him and with him, we may go to the Father.

One man whose entire life was turned around by an encounter with Christ was the apostle Paul. In this chapter we reflect on the central position the crucified and risen Christ had in Paul's life so as to understand further the meaning of Christian prayer today.

Christ, the center

Paul's conversion was not a turning from a life of sin to a life of virtue. Nor did it represent a radical shift from unbelief to faith. Paul was a committed Jew, fervently dedicated to preserving Jewish faith and practice. Because of this commitment he persecuted the early Christian Church. Then one day, by the grace of God, Paul encountered Christ in the inner depths of his being. In this extraordinary experience of the risen Christ on the road to Damascus (see Acts 9:3-19), Paul discovered that Christ *is* the Good News of salvation. Christ, not the law, is the source of eternal life.

> "I am no longer trying for perfection by my own efforts, the perfection that comes from the Law, but I want only the perfection that comes through faith in Christ, and is from God and based on faith. All I want is to know Christ and the power of his resurrection and to share his sufferings by reproducing the pattern of his death."
> (Philippians 3:9-10)

Paul did not focus on the Christ of the past, but on the risen Christ who is present now, enabling us to pray to God.

> Whatever promises God has made have been fulfilled in him; therefore it is through him that we address our Amen to God when we worship together. God is the one who firmly establishes us along with you in Christ; it is he who anointed us and has sealed us, thereby depositing the first payment, the Spirit, in our hearts.
> (2 Corinthians 1:20-22, NAB)

This Spirit empowers us to share in Christ's filial relationship with God.

> The proof that you are sons is that God has sent the Spirit of his Son into our hearts: the Spirit that cries, "Abba, Father," and it is this that makes you

a son, you are not a slave any more; and if God
has made you son, then he has made you heir.
(Galatians 4:6-7)

Paul expresses this same conviction in the Letter to the Romans:

Everyone moved by the Spirit is a son of God. The spirit you received is not the spirit of slaves bringing fear into your lives again; it is the spirit of sons, and it makes us cry out, "Abba, Father!" The Spirit himself and our spirit bear united witness that we are children of God. And if we are children we are heirs as well: heirs of God and coheirs with Christ, sharing his sufferings so as to share his glory. (Romans 8:14-17)

In Paul's theology, the Spirit of God prays within us. By the power of the Spirit we are united to the risen Christ and with him address God as *Abba*.

The Spirit too comes to help us in our weakness. For when we cannot choose words in order to pray properly, the Spirit himself expresses our plea in a way that could never be put into words, and God who knows everything in our hearts knows perfectly well what he means, and that the pleas of the saints expressed by the Spirit are according to the mind of God. (Romans 8:26-27)

Paul's focus on Christ as the center of faith and prayer gave him inspiration and strength to proclaim the Good News to the gentile world. It enabled him to endure all kinds of hardships, including imprisonment, beatings and shipwrecks (see 2 Corinthians 11:22-29). Knowing Christ was more important than anything else.

For him I have accepted the loss of everything, and I look on everything as so much rubbish if only I can have Christ and be given a place in him. (Philippians 3:8-9)

His relationship with Christ was Paul's first priority. No other reality could threaten or weaken him as long as he was secure in Christ's love.

> Nothing therefore can come between us and the love of Christ, even if we are troubled or worried, or being persecuted, or lacking food or clothes, or being threatened or even attacked. As scripture promised: For your sake we are being massacred daily, and reckoned as sheep for the slaughter. These are the trials through which we triumph, by the power of him who loved us.
>
> For I am certain of this: neither death nor life, no angel, no prince, nothing that exists, nothing still to come, not any power, or height or depth, nor any created thing, can ever come between us and the love of God made visible in Christ Jesus our Lord. (Romans 8:35-39)

Practical implications

Paul's perception indicates the central place the crucified and risen Christ must have in the prayer life of the Christian. Our God is the God of Jesus Christ. We know God through Jesus' perception; we know God by knowing Christ, who is God's Word. We go to God through Jesus Christ.

> "I am the Way, the Truth, and the Life.
> No one can come to the Father except through me.
> If you know me, you know my Father too."
> (John 14:6-7)

We pray with Christ, by the power of the Spirit, to the God whom Jesus calls *Abba*.

Nevertheless, a question remains. How, in practical terms, can we grow in prayer that is centered on Christ?

First, it is important to read and reflect prayerfully on the Gospels. Through them we learn what kind of things Jesus said and did. Further we learn of Jesus' significance for the early Christians. In this light we can come to a fuller appreciation of Christ's meaning for us today, and can better understand what he is doing and saying to us in the context of our life.

Then we can focus on the presence of the crucified and risen Christ in our lives *now*. We engage in prayerful conversation with Christ, listening to him and speaking to him in our own words. We begin to perceive the mind and heart of the crucified and risen Lord. What does Christ think and feel about the God whom he calls *Abba*? What does he think and feel about people who touch our life: family, friends, enemies? What does he think and feel about what is happening in the world today?

Through this kind of reflection we can gradually put on the mind of Christ. In touch with his inner attitude, we can pray with Christ to the God whom he calls *Abba*. We can pray for others as Christ prays for them. We can relate to others and respond to the critical needs and problems that confront society today as Christ wishes.

Conclusion

By striving to make Christ the center of our lives, we grow in the uniquely Christian dimension of our prayer which is reflected in the conclusion of the Eucharistic prayer:

> Through him,
> with him,

in him,
in the unity of the Holy Spirit,
all glory and honor is yours,
Almighty Father,
forever and ever.
Amen.

Touchstones
- How might deepening your acquaintance with the Gospels enrich your prayer life?
- Does your prayer regularly include bringing the day's events to Christ?
- What in your prayer indicates that Christ is more and more the center of your life?

Chapter ten

'According to your Word'

In the sixth month the angel Gabriel was sent by God to a town in Galilee called Nazareth, to a virgin betrothed to a man named Joseph, of the House of David; and the virgin's name was Mary. He went in and said to her, "Rejoice, so highly favored! The Lord is with you." She was deeply disturbed by these words and asked herself what this greeting could mean, but the angel said to her, "Mary, do not be afraid; you have won God's favor. Listen! You are to conceive and bear a son, and you must name him Jesus. He will be great and will be called Son of the Most High. The Lord God will give him the throne of his ancestor David; he will rule over the House of Jacob for ever and his reign will have no end." Mary said to the angel, "But how can this come about, since I am a virgin?" "The Holy Spirit will come upon you," the angel answered, "and the power of the Most High will cover you with its shadow. And so the child will be holy and will be called Son of God. Know this too: your kinswoman Elizabeth has, in her old age, herself conceived a son...for nothing is impossible to God." "I am the handmaid of the Lord," said Mary, "let what you have said be done to me." And the angel left her. (Luke 1:26-38)

Over the centuries, Christians have gone to two extremes in regard to Mary. In the first, prominent in Roman Catholicism for some centuries prior to the Second Vatican Council, devotion to Mary often obscured the central and unique role of Christ. Lost in that approach was clear insight into Mary's place within the framework of the Church.

In reaction to this some Christians have fled to the opposite extreme and denied Mary any real significance for Christians today. "All we need is Jesus Christ," they insist.

This chapter's reflection on Mary's prayer presupposes a position somewhere between these two extremes. It acknowledges that Mary herself is redeemed by Christ. It affirms that through her exemplary response to God she serves as a model of Christian discipleship for the rest of the Church. This follows the model set down by the Second Vatican Council where the bishops, rejecting a proposal to write a separate document on Mary, incorporated their treatment of Mary into the document on the Church.

In this chapter we consider four aspects of Mary's prayer that are relevant to all Christian prayer: Mary heard and did the Word of God; Mary bore Jesus Christ into the human family; Mary shared in the suffering of her son; and Mary lived a life of faith.

Doing the Word

Luke's Annunciation scene (Luke 1:26-38) describes a religious experience. In this prayerful event God calls Mary to be the mother of Jesus. Mary responds with a question: How can a virgin become a mother? Told that the Holy Spirit will come upon her, she accepts the answer with faith and gives her assent: "I am the handmaid of the Lord,...let what you have said be done to me" (Luke 1:38).

With a few strokes of his pen, Luke has captured the essence of Mary's prayer life. Mary is attuned to God's will for her. When the call first comes to her, she receives no blueprint containing the details of how everything will be accomplished or revealing all that is involved. These details will come clear only through questioning and pondering. Mary's response to the message reveals her radical openness to the Word of God; she continues to embrace all the implications as they gradually unfold throughout her life.

Mary's fidelity to the Word of God is indicated in two other Lucan narratives. In the first, Christ's mother and brothers come looking for him. When Jesus is informed of their presence he replies, "My mother and brothers are those who hear the word of God and put it into practice" (Luke 8:21).

In the second narrative a woman in the crowd raises her voice while he is speaking: "'Happy the womb that bore you and the breasts you sucked!' But he replied, 'Still happier those who hear the word of God and keep it'" (Luke 11:27-28).

These narratives point out what makes Mary Jesus' disciple: not mere blood relationship, but her embrace of God's Word. Her life of prayer centers on the Word. She listens to it, ponders it and responds by doing it.

All Christian prayer must revolve around God's Word. We hear it through Scripture, through the community of faith and through our life experiences; it echoes in the innermost depths of our heart. We ponder, meditate and contemplate. We search for the meaning God's Word has for the concrete circumstances of our life. We base our decisions on that Word, and offer as prayer our implementation of those decisions.

Mary's advice to the servants at the wedding feast in Cana exemplifies her attitude. Having brought to Jesus' attention the fact that there was no wine left, Mary instructed the servants, "Do whatever he tells you" (John 2:5). The servants followed Mary's advice—and in that context Jesus performed his first miracle.

Bearing Christ

Through her openness to God's call, Mary brought Christ into the world. Christ entered history through the mediation of Mary's cooperation with God's grace. Her yes to God's word was a yes to Christ who is God's Word. Her yes was the means through which Christ became present among humans.

Accordingly, Mary is a model for all Christians. Our yes to God involves an acceptance of Christ. By receiving Christ into our mind and heart in prayer, and by allowing Christ to penetrate our consciousness and our life, Christians give explicit and tangible testimony of Christ's ongoing presence in the world today. The crucified and risen Christ manifests his transforming and redeeming power in a visible way through the prayer-filled lives of Christians who radiate his truth, love and generous giving.

Suffering with Christ

Mary's acceptance of Christ led her to the foot of the cross. Her faith in God involved steadfast faith in Jesus despite the fact that some thought him mad and others considered him possessed. She continued to believe in him even when he was condemned by the highest authorities as a blasphemer and a political rebel. In that dark hour when the disciples fled, when one had betrayed him and one had denied him, Mary stood near the cross. She shared as only a mother and a disciple could the shame and suffering of that event.

The prayer life of a Christian brings its own vulnerability. To believe in Jesus of Nazareth as the Word of God enfleshed seems preposterous to some and sheer stupidity to others. To proclaim Christ as the absolute and definitive Savior of all humankind at times brings charges even from some fellow Christians of narrowness and arrogance. To see suffering and death itself filled with redemptive meaning in light of Christ's death and resurrection may appear a wishful projection of childhood dreams.

The Christian believes, however, that there is redemptive meaning in the suffering and shame that are sometimes involved with firm, straightforward belief in Christ. The Christian holds the hope that our life of faith and prayer finally culminates, as it did for Mary, in sharing in the risen life of Christ.

Journey of faith

From Abraham's day to our own, all human faith involves a journey. We are, after all, a pilgrim people. To strip from Mary's faith life its journey dimension does her no justice. Mary was human; she had to grow in age, wisdom and experience. She enjoyed no beatific vision in her earthly life. Nor did she possess during Jesus' growing years the theological understanding to articulate his significance as the Christ. That was only possible in the post-Resurrection, Pentecost Church.

The gradual process of Mary's growth in understanding is clearly indicated in Luke's infancy narrative. After describing the visit of the shepherds, the evangelist notes: "As for Mary, she treasured all these things and pondered them in her heart" (Luke 2:19). In telling how the 12-year-old Jesus was found in the Temple, Luke makes no attempt to hide Mary's perplexity:

> "My child, why have you done this to us? See how worried your father and I have been, looking for you." "Why were you looking for me?" [Jesus] replied. "Did you not know that I must be busy with my Father's affairs?" (Luke 2:48-49)

Mary, Luke adds, did not understand what he meant but she "stored up all these things in her heart" (Luke 2:51).

Throughout Jesus' life and ministry, Mary prayed and reflected, striving with God's grace to interpret the meaning of her son. After his death, resurrection and ascension, Mary joined the apostles and other believers in continuous prayer until the coming of the Spirit on Pentecost (see Acts 1:14; 2:1). Through the Pentecost experience Mary, with the rest of the Christian community, came to a fuller understanding of the crucified and risen Christ's true significance. The culmination of Mary's journey of faith was her own participation in the paschal event: her Assumption.

Our life of Christian faith is, like Mary's, a journey. We must work through our questions and doubts. Our faith seeks further understanding. Through heartfelt prayer and reflection we strive to discover ever more fully the significance of Christ in our lives. We struggle to determine the implications that following Christ has for us at this particular moment in our history and in the history of an ever-changing world.

Conclusion

The evangelist Luke attributes to Mary the beautiful *Magnificat*. This prayer is not a recording of Mary's actual words but a collage of texts from the Hebrew Scriptures. The author placed the prayer on Mary's lips, however, because it captures her prayerful spirit. There is no better way of concluding this chapter on Mary's prayer than by recalling these words:

> "My soul proclaims the greatness of the Lord
> and my spirit exults in God my savior;
> because he has looked upon his lowly handmaid.
> Yes, from this day forward all generations will
>   call me blessed,
> for the Almighty has done great things for me.
> Holy is his name,

and his mercy reaches from age to age for those
  who fear him.
He has shown the power of his arm,
he has routed the proud of heart.
He has pulled down princes from their thrones
  and exalted the lowly.
The hungry he has filled with good things, the
  rich sent empty away.
He has come to the help of Israel his servant,
  mindful of his mercy
—according to the promise he made to our
  ancestors—
of his mercy to Abraham and to his descendants
  for ever." (Luke 1:46-55)

Touchstones

- Does your prayer include time for reflection on God's Word as it comes to you through Scripture, the community and life's events?
- How does your prayer enable you to enflesh Christ for the people you encounter?
- Does your prayer crack the walls you have built about yourself and let you become vulnerable?
- Has your journey in prayer brought a song of praise to your lips?

Epilogue

Abraham, Moses and Jeremiah, Jesus, Paul and Mary—their prayer experiences gleaned from the Scriptures continue to speak poignantly to the shaping of contemporary Christian prayer. Each, in a uniquely personal way, illustrates the most basic biblical and theological notion of prayer: Prayer is the human response to God, who touches us and transforms us in mind and heart.

In this book we have identified some particular elements that determine the quality of this response. Prayer always involves a journey that takes us through many leavings and new horizons, dark nights and bright mornings, dyings and risings. Prayer is listening to God's Word and implementing that Word in the new and changing environs of our own history. Prayer liberates us and challenges us to engage in God's liberation of all humanity. Finally, for the Christian, prayer is response to the Spirit of God who unites us with the crucified and risen Christ, with whom we acknowledge God as *Abba* and each other as sisters and brothers. Our journey of prayer in this life culminates in that perfect union described in the Book of Revelation:

> Then I saw a new heaven and a new earth; the first heaven and the first earth had disappeared now, and there was no longer any sea. I saw the holy city, and the new Jerusalem, coming down from God out of heaven, as beautiful as a bride all dressed for her husband. Then I heard a loud voice call from the throne, "You see this city? Here God lives among men. He will make his home among them; they shall be his people, and he will be their God; his name is God-with-them. He will wipe away all tears from their eyes; there will be no more death, and no more mourning or sadness. The world of the past has gone."
>
> (Revelation 21:1-4)